DIABETES IN DOGS

A Comprehensive Guide to
Diabetes in Dogs

WRITTEN BY VETERINARY EXPERT

DR. GORDON ROBERTS BVSC MRCVS

Hello! My name is Gordon Roberts and I'm the author of this book. I hope you enjoy all of the specialist advice it contains. I'm a huge advocate of preventative care for animals, and I'd love to see more pet owners taking the time to research their pet's health care needs.

Being proactive and educating yourself about your pet's health now, rather than later on, could save you and your pet a lot of trouble in the long run.

If you'd like to read more of my professional pet care advice simply go to my website at http://drgordonroberts.com/freereportsdownload/.

As a thank you for purchasing this book, you'll find dozens of bonus pet care reports there to download and keep, absolutely free of charge!

Best wishes,
Gordon
Founder, Wellpets

Contents

Introduction

Chapter 1:
How diabetes comes about: a quick biology lesson

Chapter 2:
Knowing the causes of diabetes

Chapter 3:
The symptoms of diabetes: what to look for in your dog

Chapter 4:
How is diabetes diagnosed?

Chapter 5:
Treating your dog's diabetes

Chapter 6:
Danger signs in diabetic dogs

Chapter 7:
Managing diabetes

Chapter 8:
Feeding and exercising dogs with diabetes

Chapter 9:
Diabetes FAQs

Chapter 10:
Glossary of terms for dog owners

Conclusion

Introduction

Is your dog diabetic? Or do you suspect that he may be? If so, this book will be a great help in understanding the condition and how it might affect your pet. We'll go through all the information your vet might not have time to explain, plus all the basics in case there is anything you might have missed.

This can be a stressful time for dog owners, but don't worry. Around the world, thousands of dog owners like you are going through the same thing. Not only are they learning to cope with the added responsibilities that diabetes brings, they're also dealing with some complex biological processes and terminology. This book has been produced for normal people like you, who don't have a degree in biology or a medical qualification. It's really important that you have a solid understanding of what diabetes means for your dog and how it affects his life on a daily basis. So, we've avoided using any obscure terminology or anything that might stop you from being able to understand this complex condition. There's also a glossary of diabetic terms at the back of the book if you come across anything you don't understand.

Once you've gotten to grips with the medical side of diabetes, there's also the important task of learning to manage the illness efficiently, so that it doesn't become a burden or a source of stress. This is easier than you might think, and the section on managing diabetes contains some handy tips to help you cope.

We hope you enjoy reading this book and that it helps you and your dog to live a better life with diabetes. Diabetes can be treated and it doesn't have to mean a drastic departure from your dog's daily life and all the things he enjoys. By making some subtle changes, and being a little bit more disciplined in terms of your daily routine, you can help your dog live a long and happy life with this condition. This book will show you how.

DISCLAIMER: Whilst this book contains only medically approved advice, it is no substitute for the advice of a vet and should never be used in place of a proper medical examination.

Chapter 1:
How diabetes comes about: a quick biology lesson

Before we attempt to define diabetes, let's talk about the organ that diabetes affects: the pancreas. The pancreas is a small pinkish organ that lies in the folds of the small intestine. This small, tucked away organ has quite an important purpose: to produce the enzymes needed for your dog to digest his food.

As well as this, the pancreas produces a hormone called insulin, which controls the use of glucose (or sugar) in your dog's body. Glucose is important because it acts as the fuel, or energy source, for the cells in the body. Dogs get glucose from the carbohydrate in their meals, and it is also produced in the liver.

How insulin affects glucose

The process by which the pancreas regulates glucose is quite a complex one, but an easy way to understand it is this: there are cells in the pancreas called beta cells which produce insulin. Insulin is the substance that allows glucose to pass from the bloodstream into the cells. Without insulin, the body is unable to convert glucose into the energy it needs to do things like synthesise glycogen, proteins and fatty acids (which are important metabolic processes).

What happens without insulin?

If there is not enough insulin being produced by the beta cells in the pancreas, then there will be a build-up of glucose in the bloodstream that has no means of entering the cells and being converted into energy. This results in diabetes. Usually, excess glucose floating around the body can be reabsorbed by the kidneys, but the kidneys can only cope with so much.

Once they reach their limit, the excess glucose spills over into the urine, which is why so many dogs with diabetes also suffer from excess urination. It's also why one of the first tests for diabetes is checking the amount of glucose present in the urine. Too much glucose tells your vet that the dog's body hasn't been able to produce the insulin it needs to use up all the glucose. When the body can't use glucose for energy, it has to use fat instead. This means that a diabetic dog will also show signs of dramatic weight loss.

Human vs. canine diabetes: Understanding the difference

On a basic level, there are lots of similarities between diabetes in dogs and humans. However, it's important to note the subtle differences. Whilst dogs can develop different types of diabetes, by far the most common type they develop is "sugar diabetes" or Diabetes Mellitus, as it is known in medical terms. Dogs with sugar diabetes are not able to use the sugar in their bloodstreams efficiently.

This is because the pancreas isn't producing enough insulin (type I diabetes in humans), and not because the insulin itself simply isn't as affective as it should be (type II diabetes in humans). In fact, what we call "type II diabetes" in humans is virtually unheard of in dogs. Most dogs get diabetes because they don't produce enough insulin, rather than because the insulin they do produce is not effective.

Chapter 2: Knowing the causes of Diabetes

Now that you know a little bit more about what happens in a diabetic dog's body, you're probably wondering how the condition comes about. In this chapter, we'll go through the different causes of diabetes in dogs, from the most common to the more obscure.

Which breeds are most prone to diabetes?

Firstly, you should know that diabetes can be genetically inherited through a dog's bloodline. We know this because certain breeds are more prone to the condition than others, meaning that it has been passed down through generations. If you have a dog with diabetes, you should never breed from him or her because the chances of the condition being passed down to the pups will be high. Here are some of the breeds most prone to diabetes, according to a study carried out in the Journal of Heredity in 2007.

High Risk	Medium risk	Low risk
• Samoyed • Cairn Terrier • Bichon Frise • Border Collie • Border Terrier • Collie • Dachshund • English Setter • Poodle • Schnauzer • Yorkshire Terrier English Setter • Poodle • Schnauzer • Yorkshire Terrier	• Cocker Spaniel • Cavalier King Charles Spaniel • Doberman • Jack Russell Terrier • Labrador • Rottweiler • West Highland Terrier	• English springer Spaniel • Welsh Springer Spaniel • Boxer • Golden Retriever • German Shepherd • Staffordshire Bull Terrier • Weimaraner

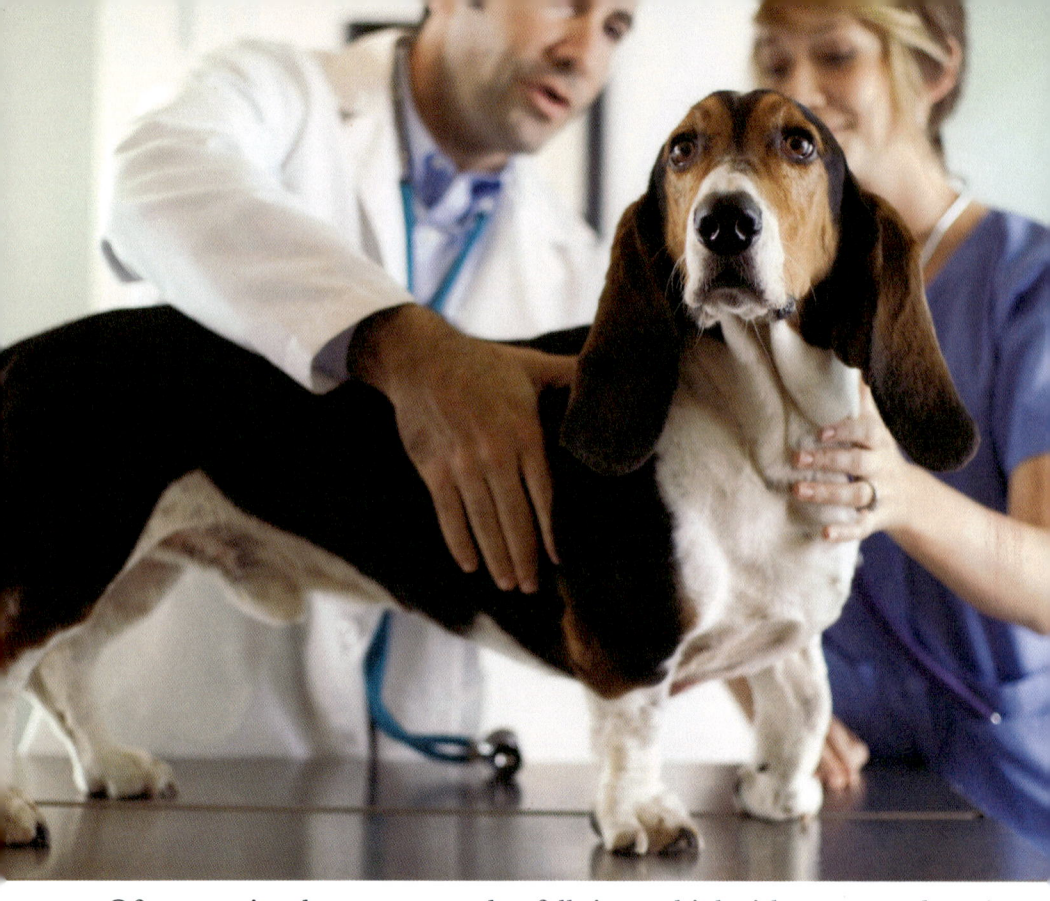

Of course, just because your dog falls into a high risk category doesn't automatically mean that they will develop diabetes. It simply means you'll need to be a bit more vigilant in terms of spotting the possible signs. If you got your pup from a reputable, responsible breeder then there's a better chance that he won't ever develop diabetes. On the other hand, there is no guarantee that he won't develop it, either. The genetic lottery can work in mysterious ways.

Age as a risk factor

Diabetes is one of those conditions which usually affects older dogs rather than pups or adolescents. It's usually diagnosed in dogs between 5 and 12 years of age. For this reason, owners sometimes dismiss the signs of early diabetes as the symptoms of old age, for example excess urination and loss of bladder control. Don't be one of these owners! Even older dogs need to be checked by a vet at the first sign of anything unusual.

Male and female dogs

According to vets, about 72% of diabetes cases are known to occur in female dogs, so we know that females are more prone to the condition than males. So what causes diabetes? Well, diabetes is quite a complex condition, so it's much more likely that a number of factors contributed to your dog developing the disease, rather than one distinct cause. It might have been a combination of genetics, environment and poor diet, for example. In reality, your vet probably won't come to a conclusive reason as to what caused the condition, but by reading up on all of the different factors you'll be able to get a fairly good idea of what applies to your dog and what doesn't.

What leads to damage in the pancreas?

What we do know is that the destruction of the beta cells in the pancreas (the ones responsible for producing insulin) usually happens over time, and is a gradual process. It is the result of a "chronic" (slow) inflammation in the pancreas. This inflammation can be caused by any of the following:

Autoimmune diseases

When there is a problem with your dog's immune system, the body starts to produce antibodies that mistakenly attack its own tissue. This happens in humans, so we know there is a good chance that it could be happening in diabetic dogs. One possible cause of autoimmune disorders is thought to be repeated vaccinations for the same disease. According to holistic practitioners, this can sometimes cause havoc with the immune system. Another cause could simply be a viral infection.

Pancreatitis

Many dogs with diabetes turn out to have a chronic form of pancreatitis, where the pancreas becomes extremely inflamed over time. The inflamed pancreas leaks digestive enzymes which, instead of breaking down food in the gut, start to break down the areas of the pancreas which are responsible for producing insulin, destroying the beta cells. This is a painful, serious condition.

Obesity

If your dog is already obese then this may have contributed to him becoming diabetic. Excess body fat tends to reduce the effectiveness of insulin, leading to a high level of glucose in the body which in turn causes diabetes. The reasons why body fat has this effect are quite complex, but one study has shown that fat cells produce a certain protein which causes the liver and muscles to become desensitised to insulin. Another study has shown that fat cells produce a hormone called resistin that causes the body to resist insulin by damaging the insulin receptors in the cells.

Diet

A diet that's too high in fat can cause pancreatitis, which in turn can cause diabetes because it leads to the destruction of the cells that produce insulin. Fatty cuts of meat and too many treats are common culprits. In addition, a diet that is too high in carbohydrates can cause sugar levels in the body to sky rocket.

Environmental factors

There are a few factors that are known to increase the likelihood of diabetes. For one thing, the amount of dogs being diagnosed with diabetes is far higher in the winter months, although we don't know why that is. Secondly, there are certain substances in your dog's environment which could be having an effect on his internal organs. One of these substances is something called bisphenol A. It is found in the coatings of dog food cans and is part of a group of substances known to disrupt certain hormonal processes, and are associated with diseases like diabetes and hyperthyroidism.

Pregnancy

Speaking of hormones, it's important to be aware that pregnancy can increase the risk of diabetes in your dog. Some dogs, especially those in their older years and at the later stages in their pregnancies, can develop a sudden form of diabetes which tends to go away once the pregnancy is over. Again, the cause is hormonal – in this case it's thought to be caused by high levels of progesterone.

Cushing's disease

Cushings disease is a malfunctioning of the adrenal glands or the pituitary gland, which results in the body creating too much of a hormone called cortisol. Cortisol has an important function to do with blood sugar and that is to keep blood sugar levels high. However, when the body produces too much cortisol, this raises blood sugar (glucose) to abnormally high levels, causing a form of secondary diabetes. So, if your dog has been diagnosed with Cushing's then you will need to be aware of diabetes as a possible complication.

Medications

Long term use of medications such as steroids and hormonal treatments are linked with diabetes because they can impair the beta cells and disrupt the production of insulin. For example, steroid medication used to treat asthma and arthritis can mimic the effects of cortisol which causes blood sugar to rise to abnormal levels.

Thyroid issues

There is a strong link between thyroid issues and diabetes. If your dog has a thyroid condition you should be especially alert to any possible symptoms of diabetes.

Abnormal functioning of the liver

Usually, when the body doesn't have enough glucose to carry out its normal functions, the liver is stimulated to produce it naturally. For reasons unknown, the livers of some dogs and humans produce glucose even when it isn't needed, which of course can result in diabetes.

Chapter 3: The symptoms of diabetes: what to look for in your dog

If you know your dog well enough then you'll probably have noticed anything untoward in terms of his general health. However, you might not have made the connection to diabetes. Lots of dog owners confuse the signs of conditions like diabetes with the signs of old age and they choose not to go to the vet. Don't be one of these owners! Look out for the following signs of diabetes and act on them as soon as possible. Also, please be aware that many of the signs of diabetes are also associated with other medical conditions, so don't fall into the trap of making your own diagnosis. Make sure to visit a vet who will carry out the necessary tests.

Urinating

Dogs with diabetes need to eliminate all that excess glucose from their bodies, and they do so by urinating in large volumes. So, if you notice your dog starts to pee a lot more than usual, and is maybe asking to be let out into the garden a lot more frequently, it could be an indicator of diabetes.

Of course, dogs with urinary tract infections will also need to urinate frequently, but they will be straining and are usually in pain, whereas a dog with diabetes eliminates quite easily, and without discomfort. The reason he is peeing so often is that the excess glucose is drawing more water into the bloodstream through osmosis. The kidneys can't reabsorb this water because of its high glucose levels, so instead they filter the water out into the bladder.

Excessive thirst

Dogs with diabetes are having to pee so often that they become constantly thirsty, to compensate for all the fluids they are losing through urinating. So if you are finding that you have to refill your dog's water bowl several times a day, they have an excessive thirst.

Weight loss

If a dog has had diabetes for a while, he is likely to be losing weight. This is because the body is no longer being provided with enough glucose as fuel. Instead of being able to use glucose to power metabolic processes, the body is forced to use fats and proteins. So, the dog's body fat will be decreasing bit by bit. It's a wise idea to weigh your dog regularly, even if he is completely healthy, so that you can easily spot this warning sign.

Over eating

Despite the fact that he is losing weight, your dog will probably show signs of overeating because his cells aren't getting the fuel they would normally get from glucose. So, to compensate for the lack of energy supply, he will have the urge to eat a lot more than usual.

However, his body will be fighting an uphill struggle because without insulin, it can't make use of all of the glucose that it's being fed. The body is being forced to use its fat supplies instead – hence the continued weight loss.

Lethargy

Once your dog gets to the stage where he's losing weight as a result of diabetes, he will also become a lot less energetic and will be sleeping more. He might be reluctant to exercise, or simply less bouncy and animated than usual.

What happens when diabetes is left untreated?

The symptoms above are just the tip of the iceberg and if you've failed to spot them and have your dog examined by a vet, they will more than likely turn into more serious issues. Note that when diabetes advances to this stage, the dog is often approaching old age and so some of the symptoms will be hard to distinguish as being caused specifically by diabetes.

So, your vet may take a little bit more time to understand what is going on in your dog's body. From your side, the best thing you can do is get your dog examined before any of these complications arise so that your dog can get early treatment before lasting damage occurs. With that said, you should be aware of the following complications with diabetes.

Toxicity

When the body is forced to break down fat for fuel instead of using glucose, the fat that is broken down releases ketones into the bloodstream. These ketones can build up to toxic levels, a condition called ketoacidosis in humans.

When this happens, dogs will feel very ill and will lose their appetites, and vomit. In this state, they will become very dehydrated and can even fall into a coma.

Eye problems

A dog that has been left untreated has a high risk of developing eye problems such as cataracts, glaucoma and even blindness. This is because the excess glucose in the bloodstream causes the lens of the eye to swell. In the early stages, your dog's vision will become blurred so you may notice him becoming disorientated, for example not spotting a treat you have put out for him.

Later on, cataracts may develop which is where the clear lens becomes cloudy and opaque, obscuring the dog's vision. You'll be able to see the cataracts if you look closely. In many cases, cataracts can be removed or corrected with surgery but it's also important to treat the root cause – the diabetes. Not every dog with cataracts has diabetes, but the two are closely linked and a large percentage of diabetic dogs end up developing cataracts.

When the eye becomes inflamed and there is a build-up of fluid, the dog can develop a painful condition called glaucoma where fluid builds up in the eye, causing pressure and headaches. Don't leave cataracts untreated as they could lead to glaucoma, which can later cause a rupture and in severe cases the eye may need to be completely removed. At the first sign of cataracts you should take your dog to the vet, even if you suspect they might be a result of old age rather than diabetes.

Bacterial Infections

Dogs with diabetes are more prone to infections, especially in the urinary tract. This is because the high levels of sugar in the blood provide a breeding environment for bacteria. You can imagine how much discomfort a urinary infection can cause a dog who is already trying to eliminate excessive amounts of urine.

For this reason, if your dog has diabetes, he should have his urine tested on a regular basis. Gum disease is also a risk, because the tartar on teeth floods the bloodstream with bacteria, which breeds faster in a body that is full of glucose. Brush your dog's teeth very regularly, ideally every day, to combat this. If your otherwise healthy dog is having recurring infections in the mouth or urinary tract, you should have him tested for diabetes.

Fungal infections

Since glucose feeds any form of fungal infestation, the likelihood of a dog with diabetes developing a fungal infection is high.

Liver disease

When a diabetic dog loses weight as a result of burning all of his body fat, it puts more strain on the liver, which is having to process high volumes of fat. Ultrasounds and biopsies can help your vet to determine whether diabetes is the culprit and how to treat the damaged liver.

Chapter 4:
How is diabetes diagnosed?

By now you should have a solid understanding of the symptoms associated with diabetes, and what to expect if diabetes is left untreated. The next obvious step is an official diagnosis from your vet. How will your vet know if your dog is suffering from diabetes, and not some other form of illness? Here are some common methods used by vets.

Medical history and symptoms

The first thing your vet will do is have a chat with you about what symptoms you've noticed in your dog. Now is the time to list anything and everything you can think of – even if you don't think it's worth mentioning. Remember that sometimes the symptoms of diabetes can masquerade as mere signs of old age. Your vet will want to leave no stone unturned when it comes to investigating your dog's symptoms. He will also ask about your pet's medical history, for example if there's been diabetes in your dog's bloodline, or if he suffers from any pre-existing conditions like Cushing's disease, thyroid problems, or cataracts.

Urine sample

If your vet suspects diabetes at this stage, he will most certainly want to carry out a urine sample. This will detect any excess levels of glucose in the urine, which the body is trying to flush from the system.

Urine samples have to be carried out in very sterile environments in order not to skew the results with foreign bacteria. However, if you are able to, you can also bring a sample with you to the vet. Just be sure you've collected it in a sterile container with an air tight lid. A diabetic dog will have lots of glucose in the urine but a healthy dog will usually show no glucose whatsoever.

Blood sample

Blood samples are also extremely useful when it comes to testing for diabetes. Healthy dogs should have about 80-150 milligrams of glucose per decilitre (one tenth of a litre) in their blood. Diabetic dogs will have abnormally high blood sugar which can reach levels of 300mg per decilitre.

If the diabetes has reached an advance stage, the blood will also show an electrolyte imbalance and it will show excess levels of ketones (a sign that large amounts of fat are being broken down in the place of glucose). Liver enzymes will also be present in higher than normal levels.

Other indicators

There is a small chance that your dog's high blood sugar might have been caused by over active adrenal glands. Although this is rare, if your vet suspects it is the case then he will want to test your dog's urine for cortisol or creatinine and other problems with the pancreas.

In addition to this, there is also something called a Frictosamine test. This test measures the amount of fructosamine in the blood, and is an indicator of the levels of glucose in the dog's blood over the past 2-3 weeks. These tests are useful when the dog's normal blood test shows only a slightly elevated glucose level, as they can confirm if the spike is temporary or something that has been going on for a while.

Making a diagnosis

Your vet will want to rule out all the other possible causes of your dog's symptoms before making a full diagnosis. However, when there is a high sugar content in both the urine and the blood, it is safe to say that your vet is probably going to make a diagnosis of diabetes. In the next chapter, we'll discuss what to do if this is the case.

Chapter 5:
Treating your dog's diabetes

You may think that diabetes sounds like a complex matter to deal with, but the treatment for this condition is fairly simple: you need to replenish the insulin that your dog's body can't produce naturally. This will help him to convert the glucose in his bloodstream into energy. With the insulin levels corrected, your dog is going to feel a lot better. Diet and exercise will also help your dog back to health. Here is some useful information about the insulin side of diabetes treatment.

Insulin treatment

Insulin was discovered in 1921. The human form of diabetes had been known to medical professionals for a long time, but it wasn't until the discovery of insulin that diabetes went from a fatal condition to something that could be managed successfully. Many of the experiments that led to the discovery of insulin were performed on dogs, so we have our canine friends to thank for the fact that diabetes is no longer a death sentence for people and pets. To give you an idea of where the insulin that we treat dogs with comes from, it is usually extracted from the pancreas of an animal such as a cow or a pig. For humans with diabetes, insulin is also produced synthetically, thanks to advances in bio engineering that were made as early on as 1978, when insulin became the first human protein to be manufactured through biotechnology.

Types of insulin

Insulin is usually given to dogs in the form of daily injections. The first thing to know about insulin treatment is that there are many, many insulin products out there which are used to treat diabetes in dogs. Reactions to these products vary from dog to dog and not every product is designed to work in the same way. So, finding the right insulin type for your dog is often an ongoing process where you and your vet monitor your dog to see what works best.

Insulin from pigs and humans are the closest types of insulin to that which is produced by dogs, and therefore the safest. Insulin from cows isn't used so much anymore, because it's a little bit different to dog's insulin and it can cause a reaction which produces insulin destroying antibodies.

The insulin your vet chooses for your dog will depend on factors like:

- How fast acting the insulin is (its "onset")
- When the insulin works the hardest (its "peak time")
- How long the insulin is effective for (its "duration")

Why peak time, onset and duration are important

Insulin needs to be administered at exactly the right time (in relation to meal times) in order to work correctly. There needs to be enough sugars in the dog's bloodstream at the time that the insulin takes effect for it to be able to perform its function. If there are no sugars in the dog's bloodstream when the insulin takes effect, it will be of little or no use to the dog because there is no glucose there for the insulin to work on in the first place. If the insulin has no glucose to act on, it will simply circulate in the dog's body without bringing any benefits. If it is administered at the wrong time, it could also cause a hypoglycemic reaction. So, timing is crucial.

Each dog will have a different daily routine and feeding times. Some dogs are fed twice a day and some are fed once a day. Some dogs have owners who are around all day and some are only home at certain times. This is why some insulin treatments have a long duration (staying active in the body for hours at a time) and some have a short duration. Just to give you some examples:

Short duration insulin acts in a very short space of time and will reach its peak activity quickly, before wearing off suddenly. A lot of the time, this type of insulin is used in emergency situations when a dog's sugar level suddenly reaches high levels and needs to be stabilised quickly.

Intermediate acting insulin reaches its peak activity between 4 and 10 hours after it is first injected (this differs between brands). It delivers a steady amount of insulin activity for 16 hours after it is first injected. Many vets split this into two separate injections.

Long acting insulin starts to work within 6-10 hours and can stay active for up to 20 hours after it has been injected. This means it provides a more consistent level of insulin throughout the day.

The science behind insulin treatment might sound complex, but don't worry, your vet will do all the hard work and will work out what is best for your dog. All you have to do is administer the insulin when you are told to, in the correct dose.

Administering insulin

When exactly you give your dog insulin and, how often, is going to be up to your vet to decide. Don't try to change the schedule or dose without your vet's advice, or you could have a very sick dog on your hands! There are two possibilities: either your vet will want you to give the insulin once a day, or twice a day. In addition, many vets will suggest that you give your dog insulin just after his meal. This is because he won't need as much insulin if he eats less than usual. There is a risk of giving your dog hypoglycemia if he does not eat but is still given insulin. Despite this, many vets still suggest giving the insulin before a meal, so that the food afterwards can be the dog's "reward". Be sure to ask your vet about these issues to put your mind at rest.

What dose of insulin will my dog need?

Each dog is different, so please don't go by what you read on forums or what your friends with a diabetic dog do. This is because:

- Some dogs continue to make a small amount of insulin on their own
- Each dog stores and metabolises insulin in its own way
- Different brands and types of insulin affect dogs in their own way

It may take several weeks for your vet to find the right dosage of insulin for your dog. In the meantime, be patient and be as proactive as you can about monitoring your dog's health. You will be asked to check your dog's blood glucose levels before meals and an hour after eating, as well as half way through the day (in the first few days of diagnosis you may need to do this hourly). To do this, you will use a glucometer which measures the amount of glucose in the blood. You can then plot a "glucose curve" (a chart) which will show your dog's glucose levels and when they peak and drop during the day. Now that your dog is diabetic, your job will be to keep these glucose levels as steady as possible, rather than having lots of peaks and troughs.

To test your dog's blood sugar with the glucometer, you will need to collect a tiny drop of blood from your dog's ear, inner lip or elbow - wherever causes the least pain. The drop of blood then needs to be analysed by the glucometer (a hand held device). The glucometer needs to be one that's made especially for dogs and not one for humans because they have a different blood chemistry. Don't worry – your dog will get quite used to having this done and if he is rewarded with a treat afterwards, he may even come to look forward to it! Once you know your dog's insulin curve, your vet will be able to devise a suitable schedule for administering the insulin.

Note that before you can prepare an accurate insulin curve, you will need to give your dog a few days for his body to get used to the insulin. The insulin curve will be more accurate if it's prepared at home, where the dog has a normal routine. In the animal hospital, your dog will be under all sorts of stress and the glucose readings won't be indicative of a normal day.

Maintaining a routine

It's important to know that when it comes to treating your dog for diabetes, a set routine is an absolute must. Exercise can affect your dog's blood sugar levels, and so can meal times. Even stress can have an effect. So, if you're going to be administering insulin based on a normal day, then every day will need to follow that "normal" routine. Exercise your dog at the same time every day (for a similar duration), and feed him at the same time every day (in similar portions). That way, your dog's insulin treatment has the best chance of working effectively.

How to give your dog insulin

One thing to be aware of when giving insulin is that it can be very easy to get distracted and give your dog too much by accident. So, always concentrate when it comes to this important part of treatment. Make sure you have the correct size of syringe and that your syringe is designed to be used specifically with the brand of insulin you're using. Otherwise, mistakes can be made.

Insulin injections are always given under the skin, most commonly to one side of your dog's spine. To minimize pain and discomfort, you should alternate sides and locations from day to day. Here are some basic guidelines to give you an idea of what to expect. Please be aware that these instructions should come directly from your vet – the following is only a rough guide.

1. Let the insulin bottle warm up to room temperature, or it could cause discomfort
2. Rather than shaking the bottle vigorously, simply swirl it around in the bottle to make sure the solution is well mixed
3. Use the syringe to withdraw the correct amount of insulin from the bottle. Be careful not to take in any air bubbles while you do this. If air bubbles do appear, simply put the insulin back into the bottle and try again. You can also try tapping the syringe to make the bubble rise enough to be expelled from the liquid.
4. Call your dog to you and lift up a fold of skin along his back, to one side of the spine. Be calm and confident when you do this, as your dog may pick up on your mood and might fidget as a result. Insert the needle of the syringe almost parallel to the line of the back, but lifted slightly at an angle, so that it goes under the skin rather than into the skin.
5. If the needle goes into the skin rather than under it, you will notice because the needle will meet with some resistance when injecting and your dog might yelp in pain. If you have a long haired dog, you may want to clip his fur to make the process easier. This will help you to see whether the needle has actually penetrated the dog's skin or not. Some dogs are more sensitive to injections than others and Terrier and Toy breeds tend to be the most sensitive. In general though, if you have inserted the syringe correctly (under the skin, not into it) then your dog won't feel much and may not even be aware that the injection was given.
6. After the injection, give your dog plenty of praise and affection. If you like you can give him a treat.

What if the insulin doesn't seem to be working?

If the insulin you give your dog doesn't lower his blood sugar levels as expected, there are several avenues to investigate. Check the following:

Are you storing the insulin correctly and is the bottle still within its use-by date?

Are you giving the correct amount, and using the right syringe?

Is your glucometer working properly? You may want to use a second one and compare the results.

What factors can affect insulin?

If you can rule out all of the above, then your vet will probably either change your dog's dosage, or put him on a different type of insulin. However, it's important to bear in mind that the following factors can also affect how your dog responds to insulin:

- Being overweight, which makes it difficult for some dogs to utilise insulin
- Certain types of insulin, such as those from cow pancreas, can cause the production of antibodies which prevent the insulin from working
- Dogs that are taking corticosteroids for an existing health issue might seem resistant to insulin, because these medications cause blood sugar to rise
- Dogs with Cushings disease might also seem resistant to insulin, because Cushings causes high levels of cortisol and thus a high blood sugar level
- If you have a female that isn't spayed, the high levels of progesterone during a heat can make the blood sugar rise and will make insulin less effective
- Pets that are anaemic or dehydrated may have a higher blood glucose reading than normal

What to ask your vet about insulin

It can seem daunting for you and your dog when you first get a diabetes diagnosis. Stay calm and focus on gathering as much information as you can to help you in the coming weeks. Remember that finding the right balance of insulin is going to take some time. Knowing what to do in an unusual situation (such as forgetting a dose) can be a huge help and will save you making emergency phone calls. So, take a pen and paper with you to the vet's and jot down the answers to the following useful questions:

- How important is it to give the insulin at a certain time of day?
- What should I do if I miss an insulin dose?
- How many hours or minutes late can I give the insulin dose?

- Should I adjust the dose if I'm giving insulin at a later time than usual, and if so by how much?
- If I gave the last insulin dose late, should the following injection be at the normal time?
- If my dog has refused to eat, should I still give him insulin?
- If my dog only eats a part of his meal, should I still give him the same amount of insulin?
- What should I do if my dog vomits his meal up, after I've given him insulin?
- What should I do if I find my dog has eaten way more than usual by accident? (i.e. he has been fed by someone else, or has been eating scraps he found)
-

Chapter 6:
Danger signs in diabetic dogs

There will be times when your dog's blood sugar isn't managed properly, or is affected by something you can't control, such as stress or a secondary medical condition. In order to be well prepared for these situations, you need to familiarise yourself with the danger signs in diabetic dogs. Here are the most important signs to be aware of.

Hypoglycemia

Hypoglycemia happens when a dog is given too much insulin and, as a result, their blood sugar drops to dangerously low levels. This can happen if:

- The dose given was too large for their current needs
- The dose given was accidentally higher than usual
- The dog hasn't eaten, so it needs less insulin than usual
- The dog has exercised more than usual, meaning it needed less insulin than was given

In dogs with hypoglycemia, the first signs you will notice are restlessness, disorientation or loss of coordination, shivering or trembling, and becoming unusually hungry. However, if the blood sugar stays low for longer and is left untreated, the symptoms will progress and the dog will become sleepy, lethargic, and will eventually lose consciousness. He may have seizures. It can very quickly become a serious condition.

In mild cases, the first thing you must do is try to feed your dog his normal food as soon as possible. Check your dog's blood glucose level with your glucometer and if the dog's levels are abnormally low, try to figure out what could have caused it. If the problem is serious and your dog is losing consciousness, you should take your dog to the vet immediately. If you aren't sure, you should make a call to your vet to see if you need to bring your dog for an examination.

If your dog is struggling to stay conscious there is very little chance of getting him to eat something. In addition, it could be dangerous to force a dog in this condition to eat as he could very easily choke. In these cases you need to have a source of liquid glucose readily available. Every owner of a diabetic dog should keep something for these emergency situations.

Here are some suggestions:
- Ask your vet to provide you with a suitable glucose solution for emergency situations
- Get some glucose tablets from your local pharmacy and dissolve them in water

In general, a dog that is hypoglycemic will need about 500mg of glucose per pound of body weight. Ask your vet for precise measurements. Some people give their dogs things like sugary corn syrup, but this contains mostly fructose, which the body needs to convert into glucose. So, these foods are slower to act. It's best to make sure you have some kind of glucose in liquid form that is ready in your cupboard for these situations.

To give your dog glucose, the best thing to do is apply it to his lips and gums, or under the tongue. Be careful when doing this as some dogs with hypoglycemia can be very disorientated and may try to bite. You can use a brush to apply the solution if you prefer. The main thing is to act quickly, and give the glucose in small amounts at a time rather than in one big dose.

Keep a close eye on your dog and as he recovers, let him eat something if he wants to. Keep in mind that the glucose will only have a very short effect and will give your dog a sugar high that will quickly wear off. So, you may need to give him more after a short time. In general though, once he is well enough to eat then the carbohydrate in his diet will replenish his glucose levels just fine. Be sure to have a proper chat with your vet afterwards to see if you can pinpoint what caused the hypoglycemia to occur.

Severe dehydration

When a diabetic dog gets hypoglycemia, severe dehydration can result. Water is literally sucked out of the vital organs such as the brain by osmosis. Water will also be lost in huge amounts through urinating excessively. The dog will become very weak and lethargic, and will lose all interest in eating or drinking. Eyes will become sunken and the skin will lose all of its elasticity.

If things are left untreated the dog will fall into a coma and there is a slim chance of recovery. However, if caught in time, the dog can be put on an IV drip and have fluid replacement therapy, as well as having things like potassium replenished.

Ketosis

You might have heard the stories about the Atkins diet, where people starve themselves of carbohydrates in order to make their bodies use their fat reserves for fuel instead. This can make people feel very sick with headaches and bad breath, and the reason for this is that it puts them in a state of ketosis. With diabetic dogs, the same can happen.

This is because without insulin, they are starved of the glucose that the carbohydrates in their diets provide. Their bodies are forced to metabolise fat instead, and when fat is broken down for fuel it produces ketones. Usually, there is always a small amount of ketones floating around in the bloodstream, but when these levels build up, they can cause a toxic level of acidity in the blood, making your dog very sick.

This condition is known as ketoacidosis and has the following symptoms:
- Vomiting
- Diarrhoea
- Dehydration
- Weakness and lethargy
- Rapid, shallow breathing
- Bad breath with an odd chemical smell

The ketones are present in the urine when this happens, and the condition can be fatal if left untreated. Often, ketoacidosis is the first sign that a dog has diabetes. Dogs with the condition need to be seen by a vet immediately, who will administer a fast acting insulin and replenish lost fluids via an IV drip.

A good way to avoid ketoacidosis is to test your dog's urine regularly to monitor its ketone levels. You can buy testing kits from your local pharmacy, or ask your vet to provide you with one.

High blood pressure

Diabetic dogs have a higher risk of developing hypertension, or high blood pressure. This can lead to kidney damage over time. You should have your dog's blood pressure checked each time you visit the vet if possible.

Nerve damage

In rare cases diabetic dogs can be prone to nerve damage, which usually presents itself as weakness in the hind legs.

Reactions with other medicines

If your dog is already on other medication, you need to be aware of any possible interference with insulin levels. Medications that affect the liver, muscle or fat tissue are especially risky, so always be sure to ask your vet if you have concerns. Corticosteroids, many of which are used to treat asthma, can interfere with the effectiveness of insulin. Antibiotics, diuretics, thyroid treatments and even aspirin can alter your dog's glucose levels so be sure to discuss these with your vet.

Chapter 7: Managing diabetes

Your dog may have been diagnosed with diabetes, but don't worry – there is light at the end of the tunnel! Whilst there is no cure, the condition can be managed quite easily with the right care and medication. Your dog can live quite a long, happy life provided he is lucky enough to have an owner who is good at managing a diabetic dog. This section will go through what exactly that involves.

A new set of responsibilities

It goes without saying that the relationship you have with your dog, and your lifestyle, are going to change slightly now that you are dealing with diabetes. However, these changes will be worth it once you see your dog regaining his health and enjoying life once more.

Some of the things you will need to think about include:

- Deciding who is going to be the person to administer insulin in your family, but making sure everyone knows how to do it
- Making sure there is always someone at home to administer insulin, at the time it is required
- Finding the right person to look after your diabetic dog if you go away for the weekend, are on holiday or you need to visit family at the last minute
- Having emergency phone numbers in place if there are any complications
- Being prepared to give a more nutritious diet, and a careful regime of exercise in order to keep your dog in good health

What you will need

Now that you have a diabetic dog, you need to prepare yourself for the various risks and emergencies that can occur from time to time.

Here is a basic list of things you will need in your diabetes kit:
- Insulin
- Syringes
- Glucose solution for hypoglycemic emergencies (when blood sugar drops to dangerously low levels)
- A medical alert tag for your dog's collar (to tell people that your dog has diabetes)
- Glucometer (a hand held device for testing blood sugar)
- Glucose test strips
- Ketone test strips
- Air tight, sterile containers for storing syringes
- A small cooler bag for transporting insulin
- Spare bottle of insulin
- Emergency phone numbers for your vet
- A responsible, experienced house sitter

You and your vet

If you are about to take on the task of managing your dog's diabetes, you need to build a solid relationship with your vet. If that means changing vets, then so be it. Your vet is going to need to be someone you trust, and someone who takes the time to explain the complexities of diabetes in simple, easy to understand language.

The vet you decide to use should ideally possess the following qualities:
- Is situated close to your neighbourhood, so that if any emergencies occur you are within easy reach of the clinic
- Has great communication skills and interpersonal skills, and is never dismissive of your concerns
- Doesn't rush through examinations because they are too concerned about a queue of people in the waiting room
- Is compassionate and friendly with your dog, rather than detached or preoccupied
- Knows a lot about managing diabetes and has experience of helping owners manage the condition

To find a good quality vet, you might want to ask other dog owners if there is someone they recommend. You could also ask at your local pet shelter, or the breeder you got your dog from. Once you have a few recommendations your best bet, if possible, is to pay them each a visit before making a final decision.

Learning about treatment

Once you have had your dog diagnosed as diabetic, be sure to ask as many questions as you need to. Don't go home wondering why you've been told to do a certain thing for your dog, or why you aren't allowed to feed them a certain food. Try to gather as much information as you need. Ask if there is a number you can call if you have questions in the first few weeks, because it may take you some time to get used to managing the diabetes.

Here are some examples of questions you may need to ask:
- How will the treatment (usually insulin) interact with other medications my dog is taking? How will it affect the health conditions my dog already has?
- What complications should I watch out for?
- What do I need to keep a record of in order to manage the diabetes properly?
- Why has the vet chosen that particular type or brand of insulin? If that type doesn't seem to be working, how long before they will try something else?
- How often does your dog need to have check ups at the vet?
- How much is the treatment going to cost? How much will the check ups be?

Remember that in the first few weeks of being diagnosed, your dog might need to have his progress monitored by the vet once every 1-2 weeks. So you will be seeing lots of each other! After a few months, once the dosage and type of insulin is correct, the need for check ups will be less frequent.

Using responsible sources

One thing to be aware of when you're researching diabetes is that there will be a huge amount of information out there which vets can't police. There are dog owners on forums claiming that certain products worked wonders for their dogs. That may be the case, but you have no way of knowing who these people are and whether their opinions can be trusted. Likewise with natural medicine and holistic treatments – there are a lot of people out there looking to make a quick buck from worried pet owners, knowing that a lot of people will try anything to make their dogs feel better.

Don't be fooled. The only opinion you can really trust is your vet's – he is the only person who has examined your dog in person and has the expertise to make informed decisions. Books like the one you're reading are fine for background information, but they should never be a substitute for visiting your vet and having a proper chat with him about your dog's health. You owe it to your dog to be responsible when it comes to these matters.

Learning to cope as a caregiver

As the owner of a pet with diabetes, you might find certain coping mechanisms more useful than others. For example, you might start to blame yourself for your dog's diabetes, and wonder if it was something you did that caused him to develop the condition. This isn't helpful – there are so many factors that contribute to diabetes, and so much we still don't know about genetics, environment, diet and even biology. Ruminating about this stuff isn't going to bring your dog back to perfect health.

In reality, the only thing that will help your dog to cope with diabetes is having an owner who is happy and healthy enough to be the best possible carer. That means keeping your stress levels low, learning to look after your own needs as well as your dog's, and knowing when to ask for support from friends, family members and your vet. Remember that this condition can be managed and there are thousands of dog owners around the world doing it quite successfully. So don't lose heart! Why not set up a support group for owners of diabetic dogs in your area? Or participate in online discussions with people who understand what you're dealing with?

Chapter 8:
Feeding and exercising dogs with diabetes

Besides treating your dog with insulin, you are going to have to make a few important lifestyle changes. One of these will be your dog's diet, which needs to be balanced and healthy. Here are some important things to know about feeding a dog with diabetes.

How important is diet in treating diabetes?

Most vets agree that diet is extremely important, not only to support the diabetes but to keep the dog as healthy as possible so that complications don't arise. Coping with diabetes is already a challenge, without having to deal with secondary health conditions, so do yourself and your dog a favour and keep your dog in excellent shape with the right diet and plenty of exercise.

Here are some important facts:
- Fatty diets, and being obese can interfere with the effectiveness of insulin
- A diet that's low in carbohydrates, high in protein with a small amount of fat can help to keep diabetes under control

Low fat

Avoid feeding your dog any foods which contain high levels of grease and fat. This can make insulin less effective once administered and it can also lead to weight gain and further health issues.

Don't be fooled by dry kibble foods – these have often been sprayed with grease to make them more palatable and to disguise some of the less tasty ingredients. The grease is often oxidised and this puts more stress on the digestive system.

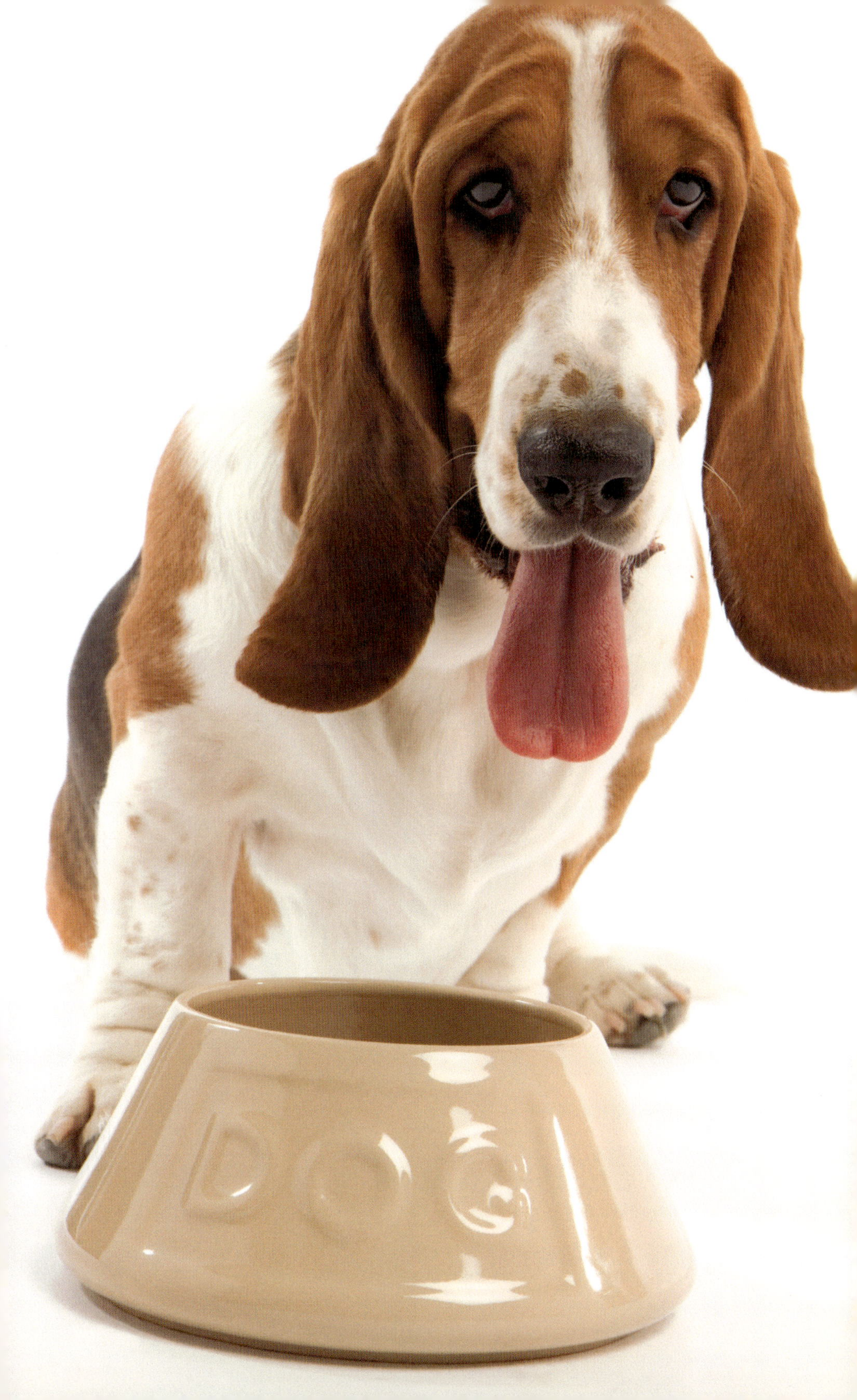
DOG

Low carbohydrate and low sugar

Avoid any foods with lots of simple sugars, or carbohydrates. There is very little evidence that dogs need carbohydrates in the first place, and by feeding them to your dog you will only be contributing to an already high blood sugar, thus worsening the symptoms of diabetes. One of the main reasons commercial dog foods contain carbs is simply because it bulks out the food and is a cheap ingredient. There is not really any nutritional value for your dog, since dogs are natural carnivores and their ancestors ate a diet purely made up of animal fat and protein.

Choose treats wisely, and give them sparingly

Treats are very useful for any dog owner because they act as a reward system for training and soothing. For diabetic dogs, treats need to be kept to a minimum because they can lead to weight gain and unwanted spikes in blood sugar. So, choose your treats carefully. Make sure they have a low calorie count, and are low in fat. Natural, rather than processed treats are a good idea – lean cuts of cooked meat, for example.

Avoid "semi moist" foods

There are some dog foods on the market that, rather than being wet, tinned food, are advertised as "semi moist". Avoid these foods as they contain some nasty preservatives and artificial ingredients which will only harm your dog. Lots of them contain dextrose, fructose and glycerin which are harmful to dogs with diabetes.

Feed a high quality dog food

When it comes to keeping a diabetic dog healthy, one of the best things you can do is to choose a high quality, nutritious food for your dog. This will keep him trim and healthy. Avoid the cheap, supermarket brands of dog food as they often contain unnecessary "filler" ingredients with no nutritional value.

Feeding schedules and diabetes

Because food is the main way your dog gets his glucose, you need to be extra careful about your feeding regimen with a diabetic dog. Feed your dog the same amount every day, at the same time every day, and you will avoid complications which arise from mistiming your dog's insulin shots. In addition to this, it's always better to feed your dog several smaller meals a day rather than one large meal, as this will help to keep blood sugar levels at an even keel, making sure they don't drop too low if the dog goes too long without food.

Conflicting opinions and research

There will be a lot of conflicting information on the subject of fibre and carbohydrates for diabetic dogs, so keep this in mind if you decide to research the topic. Remember that different dogs will respond differently to carbs and fibre, and this will also depend on the dog's weight, age, breed and size. Keep in mind that there is no standard recommended diet for every diabetic dog – your vet will need to weigh up all the factors and give you an accurate idea of the ideal diet for your dog.

What to do if your dog is obese

If your diabetic dog is overweight then it's in his best interests to try and get his weight down gradually and safely, without resorting to crash diets. You can do this simply by gradually reducing the dog's calorie intake each day. Feeding a diet that's higher in fibre can help to make the dog feel full, even if he has consumed less calories than he is used to, and will mean he doesn't go hungry. Once he has lost weight, you should find your dog's diabetes is less severe because his cells will be more able to utilise the insulin. Speak to your vet about safely reducing your dog's portion size if he is overweight – it could have an affect on the amount of insulin you need to give him.

What to do if your dog is too thin

Being underweight is a common symptom of diabetes in dogs. If your dog is underweight, be careful not to feed a dog food that's too high in fibre as anything that could interfere with his ability to metabolise food can be dangerous.

What about exercise?

In general, dogs with diabetes need the same amount of exercise as dogs without diabetes. The only difference is that the exercise itself needs to be regular and should be given at the same time every day. Your dog should ideally get the same level of exercise each day too. If a dog gets too much exercise in one day, he will need much less insulin than usual. Failing to recognise this could result in you administering too much insulin and this could result in hyperglycemia. So, you need to monitor your dog's exercise levels carefully. If, for example, he is taken on a long walk to the countryside or he meets a canine friend and they do a lot of running and chasing each other, then you may need to adjust the insulin levels of his next shot. Ask your vet if you're unsure how to proceed.

For now, you need to be aware of the following:
- Exercise uses up the glucose in the blood, as the body uses up more of it for energy to fuel the muscles and heart
- Exercise speeds up the heart rate, circulation and metabolism which dramatically increases the rate at which insulin is absorbed
- Exercise leads to a much lower level of blood sugar or glucose

In case of emergencies, it's important to bring a source of glucose with you if you're taking your dog out for an hour or more. This will help to revive him in case his glucose levels drop dangerously low, which may result in hypoglycemia.

In addition to this, you should avoid sudden changes in your dog's exercise routine. Even small changes, such as bringing him on an errand one day when he would usually stay at home, can result in low blood sugar.

Chapter 9: Diabetes FAQs

Now that you know the basics about diabetes in dogs, it's time to clear up any misconceptions you may have. Here are some answers to the most frequently asked questions about canine diabetes, which you may find useful.

What should I do if my dog goes off his food and won't eat?

Apart from raising an alarm that something is wrong with your dog, a sudden loss of appetite has a knock on effect in terms of glucose levels and insulin needs. If your dog has refused to eat and he misses a meal as a result, you will need to lower the amount of insulin you give him. Ideally, you will have asked your vet about this in advance and you will have a recommended dose for these situations written down somewhere. If not, don't panic. Remember that giving a low amount of insulin for just one day is going to be far less harmful for your dog than giving an amount that's too high (which would result in hypoglycemia). If your dog misses more than one meal, he needs to visit the vet. A loss of appetite is one of the first indicators of illness in dogs, so he will need a check up.

Why can't I give my dog insulin in tablets, instead of injections?

Some humans with diabetes can be treated with tablets. This is because they have type II diabetes, where they aren't producing enough insulin, and their bodies simply need to be stimulated to produce more of it. Dogs don't tend to have this type of diabetes – they have sugar diabetes (type I in humans), where their beta cells simply stop producing insulin altogether. Unfortunately, this means that the tablet medications that work on humans (and some cats) aren't effective enough. Dogs need to be given a direct dose of insulin into the bloodstream in order for their bodies to cope with diabetes.

Why can't I test my dog's urine for sugar, instead of his blood?

It would be much easier if you could simply rely on a urine test and a dip stick to tell you how high your dog's blood sugar is. Unfortunately, these tests aren't accurate enough to be relied on because they only measure the sugar that has leaked into the urine, and not the sugar in the blood. These are two different factors. One reason for this is that the results shown in urine can be delayed from those present in the blood. Testing the blood is an instant indicator of your dog's glucose levels, and as we've seen, timing is everything when it comes to treating diabetes. Using a glucometer is much more accurate than a dipstick, although you should keep some dipsticks or paper trips handy to measure your dog's ketone levels if needed.

Is there a chance that my dog's diabetes will go away?

Sadly with the type of diabetes dogs get, there is no known cure.

Once the beta cells lose their ability to produce insulin, this will never return. However, the condition can usually be improved quite easily with the right treatment. It's also important to note that with certain types of diabetes a reversal is possible if the diabetes is caused by something temporary, for example if the dog is pregnant, on a certain medication or suffering from Cushing's disease.

I have heard that spaying my female dog can help with diabetes. Is this true?

Spaying can help a female with diabetes, but only if nothing else seems to have worked. This is because females in heat produce a lot of progesterone, which interferes with the body's ability to control glucose levels. Progesterone can be present for up to two months after the dog has gone into heat. During this time, you might have trouble controlling your dog's blood sugar and, if this is the case, then spaying can help. It won't help to control diabetes at any other time of the year.

Chapter 10: Glossary of terms for dog owners

Diabetes is a condition that's difficult to discuss without resorting to medical terminology, so in this book we've tried to leave out the more complex terms. However, you might find this glossary of diabetic terms a useful resource when it comes to researching your dog's condition.

Acidosis
A condition where there is too much acid in the blood, usually caused by a build-up of ketones (produced when diabetics burn fat instead of glucose)

Adrenal glands
Two glands located on top of the kidneys. These glands make stress hormones which affect the body's metabolism of carbohydrates.

Antibodies
Proteins that the body produces in order to attack foreign bodies such as bacteria. When the wrong type of insulin is used on dogs, it can produce an antibody reaction

Beta cells
These cells are located in the pancreas, in an area called the islets of Langerhan. They produce insulin which controls the level of glucose in the blood.

Carbohydrate
One source of energy that comes from your dog's food, in the form of sugars and starches that are broken down to form glucose.

Dextrose
A type of glucose that's derived from starches, and is used quite a lot in processed foods like syrups

Euglycaemia or Normoglycaemia
These terms describe the state of having a normal blood glucose concentration

Fructose
A kind of sugar that is found in fruits, vegetables, honey and artificially sweetened foods. Fructose isn't recommended for diabetics as it can have a negative effect on blood sugar.

Glycemic Control
The phrase used to describe the act of controlling the levels of glucose in the bloodstream

Hyperglycaemia
A condition where the levels of glucose in the blood (the blood sugar) are too high

Hypoglycaemia
A dangerous condition where the level of glucose in the blood falls dangerously low. Symptoms include weakness, trembling, vomiting and falling unconscious

Hepatic
When something is "hepatic" it means it relates to the liver, one of the organs affected by diabetes

Polydipsia
This is the medical term for excessive thirst, one of the major signs of diabetes in dogs

Polyphagia
This is the medical term for excessive eating or an abnormally high appetite, another common symptom of diabetes

Polyuria
This is the medical term for excessive urination, which happens a lot in untreated diabetes

Post-Prandial
This term describes something that happens after food is given to your dog

Renal
Anything "renal" relates to something happening in the kidneys

Renal Threshold
The amount of sugar the kidneys can handle before the sugar begins to spill over into the urine

Conclusion

Diabetes doesn't have to be a source of stress if you manage it efficiently and are careful with your dog's daily routine. Speak to any owner of a diabetic dog and they will tell you the same thing – all of the work involved in caring for a dog with diabetes is worth it to have a happy, healthy dog.

Now that you know more about diabetes and how it can affect your dog, you should be feeling more at ease with your dog's diagnosis. The road ahead is going to be challenging, but it will get easier. As the weeks go by you'll get more and more familiar with the daily routine of checking your dog's blood sugar and administering insulin – and remember, your vet will always be there to help if you need it.

We hope you've found this book useful and that you will keep it to refer back to whenever you need it throughout your dog's life. We wish you and your dog the very best.

Want to know more about looking after your pet?

The writer of this book, Dr. Gordon Roberts, is a veterinarian and owns a total of eight animal hospitals around the UK. He believes that the key to a healthy, happy pet is preventative care, which is only possible when pet owners take the initiative to educate themselves about their animals. As a result, Gordon has written dozens of useful reports on pet care in order to share his years of experience with discerning pet owners. As a thank you for purchasing this book, you can browse and download his specialist reports completely free of charge! You'll learn all sorts of useful information about how to spot possible health conditions early on, and how to make preventative care for your pet a priority, helping you save time and money on visits to the vet later on. To view and download these bonus reports, simply visit Gordon's website at: http://drgordonroberts.com/freereportsdownload/.

Best wishes,
Gordon

Printed in Poland
by Amazon Fulfillment
Poland Sp. z o.o., Wrocław